TURN YOUR DREAMS INTO REALITY

The power of ambition for professional success

Written by Sophie Vercruysse
Translated by Rebecca Neal

Can success arrive suddenly, when the person is not expecting it?

Is there an age limit for professional success?

DEVELOPING THE REFLEXES FOR SUCCESS

- **Issue:** how can I turn my dreams into reality in order to thrive professionally and take control of my own destiny?
- **Uses:** ambition is a driving force which pushes us to want the best for our future. We just need to know where to start and put a plan of action in place to turn our dreams into reality!
- **Professional context:** career management, management, career change, starting a business, etc.
- **FAQs:**
  - Does success only depend on the individual?
  - How can I surround myself with the right people to increase my chances of success?
  - Do you need to trust your instincts in order to succeed?
  - Is it possible to be ambitious while respecting the values of altruism, empathy and generosity?
  - Does an ambitious person necessarily need to be sure of themselves and free of inhibitions? What knowledge is necessary for success?
  - How can I bounce back and succeed after a series of failures in my private or professional life?
  - How can women develop their ambition? Isn't ambition primarily a male domain?
  - Is it necessary to have a lot of money in order to succeed?
  - Can success arrive suddenly, when the person is not expecting it?
  - Is there an age limit for professional success?

> "Success is not the key to happiness. Happiness is the key to success. If you love what you are doing, you will be successful." (Albert Schweitzer, humanist and winner of the Nobel Peace Prize, 1875-1965)

Nowadays, social and professional success are paramount. They are a way of showing who you are to yourself and other people.

In order to make your dreams come true, you can take inspiration from people who have already reached their goals. The media and social networks are brimming with exciting stories from daring people who seem to have it all. For example, there is Olivier who had no qualifications but was able to launch a tech startup which is constantly growing. There are also inspiring stories about career changes: Cécile used to work in advertising and now manages her own restaurant (Les Nouveaux Audacieux, 2015). And of course, we also witness admirable rises within companies, such as a colleague who has climbed the ladder at the company and is now in a senior position.

How did these people go about achieving their goals? What is their secret? Is it luck or destiny? It must quickly be recognised that this is not the case: although luck can be useful, it has little bearing on long-term success. How, then, can you have one of these perfect careers? How can you realise your dreams? How can you bring your ambitions to life and take control of your destiny?

There is an undeniable link between ambition and success. As a general rule, ambition is to do with attitude and is the essential ingredient that leads to success. Nonetheless, success is also a matter of courage and opportunities, or rather the creation of opportunities. It never happens by chance. Although first of all you have to dream it – this is where ambition comes in – you also have to plan it, develop it and build it. To do this, there are a number of techniques which let you clarify the goals you have set and move towards them step by step.

Furthermore, although you need to put a plan of action in place, you also need to follow your intuition: that little inner voice is often insightful. It talks to us about our deepest aspirations in life and the things that excite our emotions, and refers to our values. Indeed, there is no point setting a fantastic goal for ourselves if it does not match up with who we really are.

If you want to give life to a project, finally realise your dream and accomplish your deepest aspirations, this guide is for you. Thanks to a few useful keys for drawing on your resources, it will help you to see more clearly and formulate strategies to achieve your goals.

POSITIVE AMBITION: THE BASICS

In terms of etymology, ambition comes from the Latin word *ambitio*, which means "to go around" (*amb*: around and *ire*: to go). According to the Collins English Dictionary, ambition means "strong desire for success, achievement, or distinction".

A word with two meanings

Although ambition is widely used in everyday language, it is nonetheless a somewhat ambiguous word which covers several concepts. The term "ambition" may also have negative connotations because it is sometimes seen as the opposite of humility and modesty. In this usage, ambition is classed as a form of brash arrogance.

In his book *L'Ambition ou l'épopée de soi* ('Ambition or the Epic of I'), the French philosopher Vincent Cespedes bases his definition of ambition on the work of the French historian Jules Lacroix de Marlès. According to this 19th-century author, we must differentiate between two kinds of ambition. One is lofty and generous almost to the point of magnanimity, whereas the other is dark, jealous, anxious, vulgar and insensitive to the instruments it uses to achieve its ends. Cespedes concludes that these two types correspond to the two moral poles of good and evil, and asks whether, in our selfish and nihilistic age, it is possible to rediscover positive ambition.

Towards creative ambition

This philosophical and moral perspective is important to better define the framework that this guide fits into. We are focusing on this positive and altruistic form of ambition, which is a force that creates energy and is the driver behind dreams, courage and achievement, and is both personal and collective. The French philosopher Michel Onfray (born in 1959) has also contributed to the rehabilitation of the term. According to him, "ambition is the legitimate desire to achieve one's ends in a reality in which the rules are respected"[1] (cited in Jacob and Auroux, 1990).

In this guide, you will get to work based on this positive outlook stripped of its flashy, egocentric aspects. Take a big sheet of paper, a pencil, an eraser and some Post-it notes, and make yourself comfortable somewhere nice and calm!

LET YOURSELF DREAM

This first step involves letting your imagination run free to answer the question: what do you dream of doing in or with your life?

Passion and positivity

Choose a time when you are feeling good to answer this question, because you must think about what you really want. Your answer must not involve thoughtlessly fleeing from your current situation because you no longer want to

---

1. This quotation has been translated by 50Minutes.com.

be part of it. The ability to look to the positive is of central importance here, but will also be crucial throughout the process. Cultivating positive emotions allows you to keep your attention focused on your goal, whereas negative emotions such as anxiety, fear, doubt, guilt, demoralisation and powerlessness will have a paralysing, destructive and energy-sapping effect.

At this stage, the only constraint is that you must think of activities that can make you happy. You absolutely have to like the objectives you set, because this will shape the motivation you need to pursue them. Let yourself dream and get excited!

Harmony and balance

Feel free to draw up columns to distinguish your professional objectives from those that are more personal to you, such as aspects of your personality that you want to develop. Take this opportunity to add more private aspects linked to your family, your partner and your hobbies. Your private and professional life really form one whole, and you must reconcile all these elements to achieve overall harmony.

Things to think about

What would be my dream job?	Opening a gourmet restaurant
Where would be my dream place to work?	On the Côte d'Azur
What do I expect from my private life? (Partner, children, friends)	• Live with a partner and have children • Meet new people
With regard to my passions, what are the things that I dream of doing?	• Discover Argentina • Write a book • Do a parachute jump
What are the talents and skills I would like to develop?	• Take photography classes • Learn Spanish

Clearly formulating your objectives makes them real. Putting them into words is the first step towards turning your dreams into reality, because this transforms them into tangible goals. By verbalising your dreams, you change them from abstractions into reality.

DEFINE YOUR AIMS

Once you have finished this work, focus on your professional objectives. You will be able to analyse your other goals later.

Authenticity

Take a step back and ask yourself if your goal is really personal. This is about differentiating between an attractive idea and a goal that you think about constantly, that gnaws at you and that you cannot imagine your future without. If it is something you think about all day long, it will be worth holding onto it and doing everything you can to make it a reality. An effective exercise to know if you have set the right goals is to envisage yourself in the future and note the emotions you feel when you imagine achieving your aim.

Two methods of analysis

The SMARTE method and a SWOT analysis will give you specific and very rich perspectives to clarify the goal you are aiming for and the framework it fits into.

- The SMARTE method is commonly used in project management and as part of professional development. It allows you to clearly define an objective in order to achieve it. An objective is considered to be SMARTE when it is:
  - **S**pecific, meaning that the objective must be precisely formulated and adapted to your personal context.

Question	Example answer
What needs to be done?	Find a job as a web designer
Why is it important to do it?	To earn a living and thrive professionally
Where should/can it be done?	In the non-profit sector
Who is going to do it?	Me
When does it need to be done?	As soon as possible, but I am giving myself three months to do it
How can it be done?	By applying, by increasing contact with potential employers and by going to events where I could meet them

Turn Your Dreams into Reality © 50MINUTES.com

- ○ **M**easurable, meaning that you must be able to quantify it. To do this, you must clarify the relevant indicators which will show that the objective has been reached. This will also allow you to set intermediate goals.

Question	Example answer
What measurable actions can I take?	• Respond to five job adverts per week • Send five speculative applications per week (look for contacts, invitations and information about companies on Facebook and LinkedIn) • Sign up to LinkedIn and post twice per week • Follow up on applications • Go to one event per week where I could meet possible employers • Work on my English: five hours per week

Turn Your Dreams into Reality © 50MINUTES.com

◦ **A**chievable in the time given.

Question	Example answer
• Is the objective achievable in the time allocated? • Do I have the resources I need to achieve it? • Do I have a good understanding of the limits and constraints? • Has someone else already managed to accomplish this?	In theory, I am fully capable of getting a job as a web designer in three months. I have the necessary qualifications and some relevant experience. When I get my English back up to scratch, I will have all the skills required. I am organising myself to have the time to apply and be active in my virtual and physical networks while simultaneously carrying out other activities.

◦ **R**ealistic, meaning relevant and directly linked to the person who must implement it. It can be ambitious, but it must remain reachable, and you must ask yourself if you have the abilities, skills and qualifications necessary to reach your goal.
◦ **T**ime-bound, meaning that there is a precise deadline or time frame. Indeed, an objective with no deadline will tend to be pushed back and to spread out across time, or even to never be accomplished. It is also possible, and recommended, to set yourself intermediate deadlines.
◦ **E**thical, meaning in line with your values. You must determine the true motivations that are pushing you to act and ensure that they are ethical and really fit in with your values.

- Next, a SWOT analysis is an excellent tool to analyse an objective in its entirety. This method allows you to quickly analyse the overall framework that your goal fits into. This framework comprises internal elements linked to you (strengths and weaknesses) and external elements related to the environment it falls into (opportunities and threats). When you are filling in the table, take care to order the elements in descending order of importance and indicate a maximum of three to five elements so that you can clearly interpret the results.

Example of a SWOT analysis for a web designer

Strengths (S)	Weaknesses (W)
• Good knowledge of web languages and tools • Bilingual: French and English (technical) • Interest in new technologies	• Poor knowledge of Dutch • Will have to outsource some IT aspects to a developer • Little experience
Opportunities (O)	Threats (T)
• Growing sector • New markets: ecommerce, apps • Development of social media	• Lots of competition • Very quick evolution of technology • Simplification of tasks: new platforms which allow companies to create their website themselves

REACH OUT

As soon as possible, you need to meet people working in the sector you are targeting, look at similar projects and ask questions to experts in the field. Get out of your bubble! Talk genuinely about your project without going into detail.

Create a pitch for your project

Before contacting anyone, prepare for your interviews and write a very brief presentation (no more than one or two minutes), either about your project or about you. You can draw on the elevator pitch; below is one possible template.

- **Identification:** "Hello, I'm... and my project is called..."
- **Problem:** "Have you ever noticed that..." or a brief story (very short)
- **Target:** "... is for anyone who..."
- **Service provided:** "... and it lets you..."
- **Needs:** "To launch... I need..." (financing, experts, etc.)
- **Reminder:** "Thank you for listening, here is a reminder of the name of my project..."

This stage will allow you to bring your idea face to face with reality, to fuel your reflections and to meet experts, potential employers and even your first customers if you are looking to set up a business.

SCARED THAT YOUR IDEA MIGHT BE STOLEN?

It is possible that other people have already thought of, are currently thinking about, or will think of your inspiring idea. This will only prove that you are on the right track. Do not worry too much because, unlike them, you are no longer at the dreaming stage. You are giving yourself the means to reach your goal. You have already taken a major step. Ideas, even very good ideas, have no value in themselves: it is your personality and the way you go about carrying them out that will make you stand out from other people. Nonetheless, if your idea is truly innovative, research the legal means that will allow you to protect it (patent, trademark registration, copyright, etc.).

Immerse yourself in the atmosphere

Walk around a shop like the one you want to open. Feel the atmosphere of your dream restaurant and talk to the owner. Go into the company you want to apply to work for. Talk to people who are doing your dream job. How do you feel? Does it suit you? What would you do differently? This immersion will give you a wealth of valuable indications and, as well as bringing you face to face with reality, will allow you to establish your first professional contacts.

Build your network

In the era of the internet and social media, it is easy to maintain contact with a large number of people, including those you would have struggled to approach previously.

Your network includes both people close to you (family, neighbours, friends, former colleagues) and people connected to your sphere of activity (experts, journalists, politicians). Do not hesitate to seize every opportunity to expand your circle of acquaintances. Every situation can bring you into contact with new people, and social networks allow you to prolong and maintain this contact.

The advantage of a network is that it can save you a lot of time in multiple areas: making a connection, obtaining information, getting a helping hand, opening up new horizons, etc. They are based on solidarity and exchange. Think about what you can offer other people and do not forget to thank those who have helped you.

The SWOT analysis will have allowed you to highlight the major skills that you have to direct your project, as well as the contextual elements that are favourable towards this goal. Now you need to lay out all your other assets and believe in your ability to use them at the right moment.

Feed on your success

A good exercise to strengthen your self-belief is to remember the challenges that you have already managed to overcome: doing well in a difficult exam, successfully completing a personal project, situations where you acted courageously, etc. Remembering your willpower, perseverance and motivation will drive you to take on new trials and once again surpass your limits.

Surround yourself with the right people

Listen to relevant and constructive advice which will help you to set off in the right direction, but avoid negative information. Stay away from media which disseminates fear and from people who are defeatist and negative. It's a safe bet that they are projecting their personal fears and their own inability to believe in themselves. Protect yourself and, if you need to, find someone who can coach you to hold your course.

DRAW UP A PLAN OF ACTION

Identify the resources you need

The SWOT analysis will have shown some abilities or skills that you lack, as well as external factors that are less favourable to your project. That does not matter: you will need to find the missing information, undertake training and identify the professionals or bodies that will give you the tools you need. Consequently, you should draw up a list of all the tasks, resources, training, information, reading and professionals that you will need to successfully complete your project.

Set yourself deadlines

You need to quantify the amount of time you need to reach your goal and establish intermediate steps to achieve it. Each step should be formulated using the SMARTE method.

Examine all the elements from all sides and draw up your plan of action. Set yourself precise deadlines and stick to them, because if you are not careful day-to-day life will soon catch up with you and move you away from your goals.

What	How	With (who)	For when	Done (tick)

Set a budget

After this clarification, it will be easier for you to define the resources that you need. Think about every aspect of the question, because you will need to establish a precise budget. How much does training cost? What investments will be unavoidable to put my project in place? Do I need to plan for moving? Should I set up a financing plan? How much money do I need to live on?

MOVE ON TO ACTION AS SOON AS POSSIBLE

Do not wait until you have gone through all the stages before starting your market research, testing your products and offering your services. If you have not yet finished your training, this is not a problem: research which employers you could apply to. Meet them. Offer to do an internship at their company. If you want to start your business, do not wait until your website is ready: talk about it on social media instead. Do not wait to sell. Your first customers will bring you a wealth of valuable information on the profile of your clients, their needs, how they work and how you can reach them.

Get out of your comfort zone and think about everything you can put into action starting today.

NEVER GIVE UP, EVEN IF YOU FAIL

Motivation, passion and perseverance are essential fuels if you want to make progress. Congratulate yourself on each step you complete and each success, while continuing to take care of yourself and being kind to yourself. Every day, draw up a quick list of everything you have done during the day and emphasise the positive aspects.

Start your day by working on a task which is essential to your project, even if it is only for ten minutes. Some people like to do the thing they find most boring first in order to avoid procrastination. Conversely, others prefer to start the day with a task they like in order to better tackle tedious activities afterwards. Whatever method motivates you, the important thing is to spend some time every day working on tasks with a high added value. This reflex will enable you to make faster progress and to redirect your actions more quickly if they have not paid off.

If you encounter failures, do not view them as failures. Draw lessons and knowledge from these trials. They indicate that you should change your tactics and redirect your approach.

When you achieve one of your objectives, set yourself another, but without becoming obsessive about it. Know when to let go and temporarily step away from your dream. This will give you some breathing space and allow you to come back more relaxed and receptive. It will also encourage creativity, which needs freedom to emerge.

TOP TIPS

- To realise your ambitions, you will need to identify, tame and overcome your fears. A good way to put them into perspective is to focus on the here and now. Mindfulness mediation is an excellent way of doing this.
- Adopt a positive attitude, because the image you reflect will influence the way you perceive yourself and the way others see you. Smile, and turn towards smiling people who appreciate you!
- Make sure you take care of yourself and cultivate kindness towards yourself. Try to regularly step away from your project, clear your mind, do some sport, spend quality time with your family and see your friends. These activities will revitalise you and enable you to stay on course.
- Use the right social networks and avoid mixing your private and professional lives too much. Make sure you fix the privacy settings on your profiles so as to control the image you give of yourself online, and present your profiles in accordance with your areas of interest.
- Draw lessons from your failures and be kind to yourself when they happen. Do not remain frozen and wounded, and do not lose heart. Try to look your failures in the face and understand them. A failure can become a guide or a springboard to new opportunities.
- Think about the people who can serve as role models for you and learn from their example. Try to meet them and talk openly with them. You will be able to benefit from their experience and their informed advice.
- If you lack self-assurance, know that it is possible to learn

to assert yourself at any age. Work on your posture, the image you convey, your way of speaking, your way of presenting yourself, etc. If you need to, take advice from a specialist in this area. You could try finding a professional coach who will help you to develop your objectives and work on your self-confidence.

- Learn to seize opportunities when they arise. If you've heard that someone is looking to complete their team, offer your services. If you come across a person who could help you, do not hesitate to approach them. Do it without being afraid: the worst that can happen is that they could say no. Learn how to leave your ego to one side and stop worrying about how other people see you. These are the attitudes that will lead you towards freedom.
- If you have set your goals too high or not high enough, redefine them along the way so as not to lose your motivation. Keep paying attention to yourself and to your situation, because this can change from one day to the next. In this case, alter your approach quickly.
- Keep moving forward! Each step, no matter how small, will bring you closer to your dream. Do not waste too much time asking useless questions. Simply get started and act, and you will see that opportunities will present themselves more easily.

FAQS

DOES SUCCESS ONLY DEPEND ON THE INDIVIDUAL?

There are a number of factors that largely depend on the individual: ability to seize opportunities, courage, willpower, creativity, ability to move past failures, ability to question oneself, ability to redirect the project, etc. Nonetheless, some factors remain outside the will of the individual: health, traumatic events, type of society, age, sex, etc. Even if you can always use creativity to get around difficulties, you obviously cannot decide on everything and external events can of course have repercussions which must be taken into account. The essential thing is to be able to adapt and bounce back from difficulties or failure.

HOW CAN I SURROUND MYSELF WITH THE RIGHT PEOPLE TO INCREASE MY CHANCES OF SUCCESS?

To successfully complete a project, you must come out of isolation. It would be ideal to join a group of people who share the same dynamic. Collective emulation enables you to take big steps forward and to exchange best practices, but also to compare your ideas to other people's. Furthermore, developing a professional network will form an important base for your activity.

A professional coach will also be able to offer an informed

opinion on your project and guide the decisions you need to take. In this case, as when choosing any professional (business partner, accountant, legal expert, etc.), you must make sure of their skills, but also find someone who you can trust and who you get along well with.

DO YOU NEED TO TRUST YOUR INSTINCTS IN ORDER TO SUCCEED?

The trend towards rationalisation has gradually sidelined the role of instinct. As instinct is not based on any tangible element, we often give it little credit. However, it is a powerful sense which can be a very good indicator for those who know how to use it. In fact, it can guide you on the decisions you need to take. You need to know how to listen to the little voice inside you, because often the first solution you come up with is the best one. Nonetheless, you must always make sure that you have a good understanding of the situation and take care not to confuse your desires for intuition.

IS IT POSSIBLE TO BE AMBITIOUS WHILE RESPECTING THE VALUES OF ALTRUISM, EMPATHY AND GENEROSITY?

Ambition gets bad press when it is associated with individualistic values (pushiness, selfishness, lack of solidarity or empathy). Nonetheless, when it is guided by the nobler values of self-fulfilment within a community, it is the driving force behind great works which can benefit all of humanity. Think, for example, of the winners of the Nobel Peace Prize: the values of humanism and altruism have guided them and led them to the end of their fight.

Ambition which is noble and respects others can really move mountains and bring out the best in mankind. Pay attention to your values, as they have the power to turn a dream into reality.

DOES AN AMBITIOUS PERSON NECESSARILY NEED TO BE SURE OF THEMSELVES AND FREE OF INHIBITIONS? WHAT KNOWLEDGE IS NECESSARY FOR SUCCESS?

Self-confidence is an asset, but it is not essential. A shy or reserved person can definitely succeed and get to where they want to go. Plenty of other qualities are necessary: determination, perseverance, the ability to seize opportunities, organisation, courage, resilience (the ability to bounce back after a setback), creativity, knowledge of your field, trustworthiness, passion, determination, etc.

Nonetheless, the success of a project can help someone who was initially reserved to become more sure of themselves. Supervision by a professional coach will allow the person to work on their self-assurance by showing them all the challenges they have overcome and leading them to congratulate themselves for this.

HOW CAN I BOUNCE BACK AND SUCCEED AFTER A SERIES OF FAILURES IN MY PRIVATE OR PROFESSIONAL LIFE?

It is sometimes difficult to get back on your feet after a failure. If the incident is too painful, some people react by feeling guilty, others fall into denial, and some become aggressive. All these attitudes constitute an attempt to run away from the problem rather than facing up to it.

By shouldering your responsibilities and drawing lessons from your mistakes and failures, you also learn about yourself, others, and the methods you can use to get past the situation. Developing this faculty for resilience will save you time and give you the insight you need to change your tactics.

Take the American manufacturer Henry Ford (1863-1947), for example. He went through five failures before launching his automobile company. He said that "Failure is simply the opportunity to begin again, this time more intelligently" – a great lesson in perseverance!

HOW CAN WOMEN DEVELOP THEIR AMBITION? ISN'T AMBITION PRIMARILY A MALE DOMAIN?

Nowadays, the majority of women aspire to fulfilling jobs and aim to control their own lives. Although sexist stereotypes and divisions still exist and women remain underrepresented in some senior and powerful positions, the women's cause has already made many advances.

The major challenge for women at present is to reconcile their private and professional lives without sacrificing one part for the other. A turning point has been reached and, step by step, women are taking control of their own destinies and moving into fields of expertise that were once the sole preserve of men.

IS IT NECESSARY TO HAVE A LOT OF MONEY IN ORDER TO SUCCEED?

If you want to make progress in your career as an employee, there is no need to spend money. However, it will be difficult to avoid spending money if you are an entrepreneur. Nonetheless, you do not necessarily have to have enormous sums at your disposal: to start with, a few thousand pounds of your own funds is generally enough. This personal financial investment will show that you are prepared to risk your own money to undertake your project. For the rest, you can ask for credit from financial institutions.

The key, then, is to carefully study the financing plan, your personal needs, your break-even point, etc. In short, you need to establish realistic predictions and have a cast-iron business plan!

CAN SUCCESS ARRIVE SUDDENLY, WHEN THE PERSON IS NOT EXPECTING IT?

Success very rarely arrives alone. The conditions that you create will encourage success. In general, there is little connection between chance or luck and long-term success. Nonetheless, if favourable circumstances take shape, you must seize the opportunity rather than letting it pass you buy.

IS THERE AN AGE LIMIT FOR PROFESSIONAL SUCCESS?

You can achieve great things at any age. There is no limit to that, other than the brakes you put on yourself and the way that you view yourself. As long as you have good health and enough determination, you can always decide to reinvent yourself in a new field, to follow your passion and to live the life you have always dreamed of.

OVER TO YOU

You now have a selection of tools to get started and progress step by step in your reflection. Keep your final objective (your dream) in mind, because this will give you the motivation you need to keep going in case of setbacks. If you need to, create a little positive visualisation board to picture yourself in your ideal future. This is made up of pictures, photos and symbols which represent what you want.

Of course, you will encounter obstacles throughout your journey, but after each little victory, congratulate yourself or celebrate it with those close to you.

You can use the summary chart below as a guide. Put it up somewhere to give yourself an overview and see where you are in the process.

Finally, do not forget to change your ideas, clear your head and do some sport. Creativity comes when you let go, step aside and take some distance. Do not feel guilty if you do not spend every moment working on your project – taking time off will help you make faster progress!

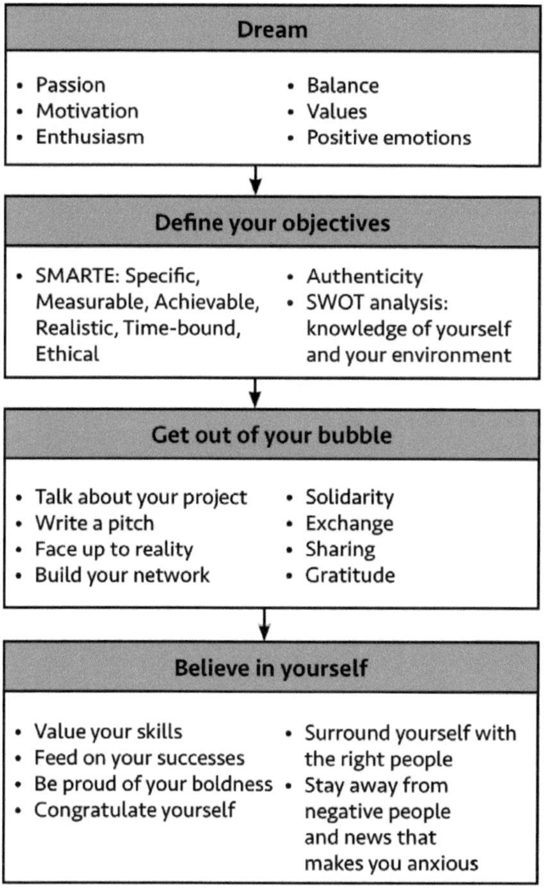

Dream

- Passion
- Motivation
- Enthusiasm
- Balance
- Values
- Positive emotions

Define your objectives

- SMARTE: Specific, Measurable, Achievable, Realistic, Time-bound, Ethical
- Authenticity
- SWOT analysis: knowledge of yourself and your environment

Get out of your bubble

- Talk about your project
- Write a pitch
- Face up to reality
- Build your network
- Solidarity
- Exchange
- Sharing
- Gratitude

Believe in yourself

- Value your skills
- Feed on your successes
- Be proud of your boldness
- Congratulate yourself
- Surround yourself with the right people
- Stay away from negative people and news that makes you anxious

Establish a plan of action

- Identify the resources you need
- Set deadlines
- Budget

Take action

- Test your services or products
- Don't wait to get started
- Be proactive
- Leave your comfort zone

Never give up

- Fuels: motivation, passion
- Congratulate yourself
- Be kind to yourself
- Avoid procrastination
- Turn your failures into experiences
- Let go
- Breathe
- Change your ideas

FURTHER READING

BIBLIOGRAPHY

- Bérubé, M. and Vachon, M. (2010) *Oser changer. Mettre le cap sur ses rêves.* Éditions Oserchanger.com.
- Cespedes, V. (2013) *L'Ambition ou l'épopée de soi.* Paris: Flammarion.
- Cintrat, F. (2014) *Comment l'ambition vient aux filles? Des histoires vivifiantes. 15 trucs et astuces pour réaliser ses ambitions.* Paris: Eyrolles.
- Filliozat, I. (2015) *Petit cahier d'exercices pour se relever d'un échec.* Chêne-Bourg (Switzerland): Jouvence.
- Jacob, A. and Auroux, S. (1990) *Encyclopédie philosophique universelle Tome II : Les Notions philosophiques.* Paris: Presses Universitaires de France.
- Laurent, P. (2013) L'ambition n'est pas une volonté de puissance, mais la réalisation de soi. *L'Express Emploi.* [Online]. [Accessed 17 November 2016]. Available from: <http://www.lexpress.fr/emploi/gestion-carriere/l-ambition-n-est-pas-une-volonte-de-puissance-mais-de-realisation-de-soi_1301058.html>
- Les Nouveaux Audacieux (2015) Cécile, chef cuisinier. *Les Nouveaux Audacieux.* [Online]. [Accessed 17 November 2016]. Available from: <https://lesnouveauxaudacieux.com/2015/12/22/reconversion-cuisinier-cecilehatchuel-chef-publicite-lamangette/>
- Robbins, A. (2010) *Les onze lois de la réussite. De la part d'un ami.* Paris: J'ai lu.
- Tonnelé, A. (2015) *65 outils pour accompagner le changement individuel et collectif.* Paris: Eyrolles.

IMPROVE YOUR GENERAL KNOWLEDGE

IN A BLINK OF AN EYE !

www.50minutes.com